# THE PRINCE

EVIL STEPMOTHER & STEPSISTERS

in...

Raintree is an imprint of Capstone
Global Library Limited, a company
incorporated in England and Wales
having its registered office at 7
Pilgrim Street, London, EC4V 6LB –
Registered company number: 6695582

www.raintree.co.uk
myorders@raintree.co.uk

Designed by Hilary Wacholz
Edited by Sean Tulien
Original illustrations © Capstone 2016
Illustrated by Omar Lozano

ISBN 978 1 4747 1025 1 (paperback)
20 19 18 17 16
10 9 8 7 6 5 4 3 2 1

British Library Cataloguing in
Publication Data: a full catalogue
record for this book is available from
the British Library.

Printed in China.

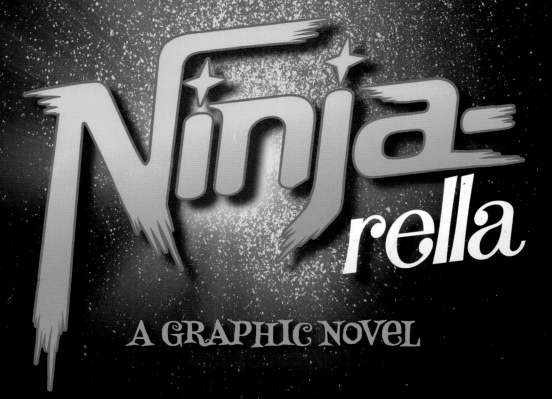

# Ninja-rella

## A GRAPHIC NOVEL

BY JOEY COMEAU

ILLUSTRATED BY OMAR LOZANO

In the beginning, Cinderella was happy. She had a family that loved her. They did everything together.

To sharpen Cinderella's mind, her mother taught her to play chess.

Her father taught her to use a sword so that she would be strong.

CLICK!

CLACK!

But one day, her mother was gone.

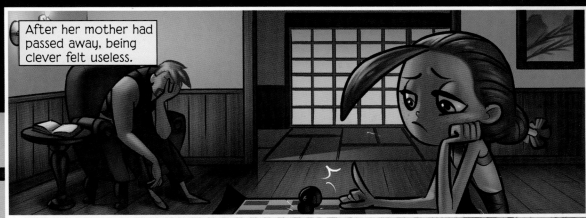

After her mother had passed away, being clever felt useless.

And being strong didn't help bring her mum back.

A short time later...

Cinderella, I've decided to get married. Meet your new mother.

My name isn't CINDER-ella, Dad. It's NINJA-rella.

It isn't healthy for a young lady to be a ninja. You should behave more like your new stepsisters.

Do they even know how to sword fight?

Do YOU even know how to be a lady?

But Ninja-rella didn't want a new mother or sisters.

So she spent her time hiding in the shadows.

Ninja-rella needed a plan...

...a way to make her father leave the evil stepmother.

But before she could come up with a plan... her father passed away.

There was nothing Ninja-rella could do. She was stuck with them.

They took away her ninja outfit and made her wear rags.

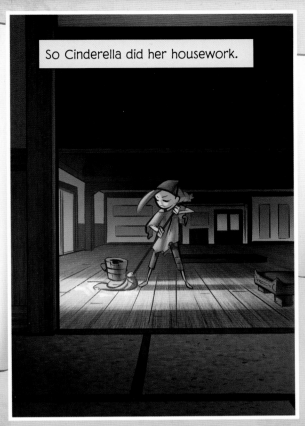

So Cinderella did her housework.

And their housework.

She did all the housework, every day, until the sun went down.

This went on for weeks.

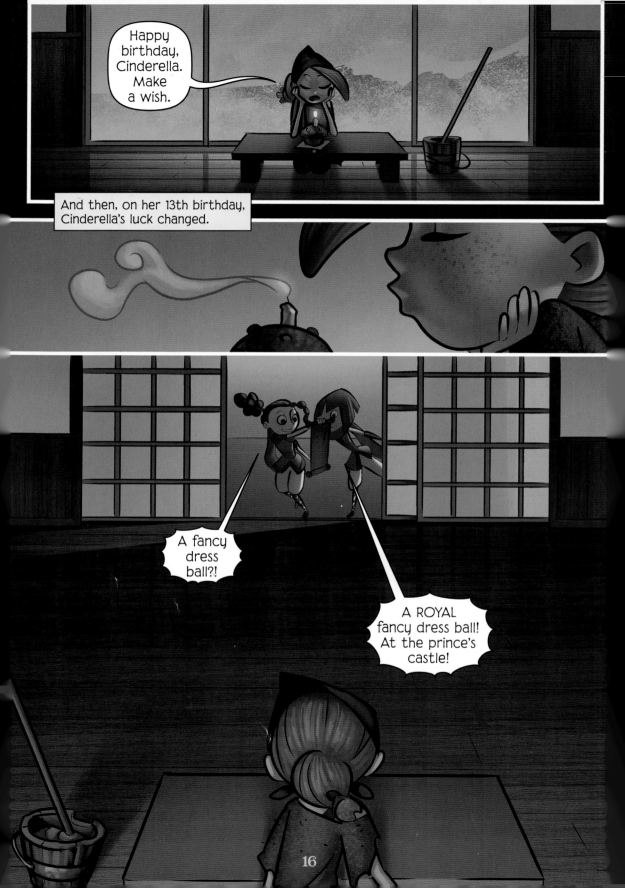

There's a party at the castle? When?

YOU want to go to a ball?

But WHY?

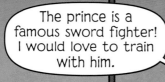

The prince is a famous sword fighter! I would love to train with him.

Good grief. Only YOU would care about something so stupid.

Don't get your hopes up. Mother will never let you go.

The next day...

WAKE UP!

So, I have decided that you will be allowed to attend the prince's royal ball.

Really?! Oh, thank you so much! How can I ever repay-

-IF you finish all the housework, and make yourself a costume by the time the ball begins tonight.

Also, your sisters will be busy trying on their dresses, so you'll have to do all of their jobs today, too.

That's not fair. I'll never get all that done by tonight.

That's not my problem. Now get to work!

So Cinderella used her ninja skills to do her housework faster than ever.

Meeting the prince was her only chance to escape from her stepmother and stepsisters.

He would see her sword-fighting skills. He would immediately employ her as his personal bodyguard.

Cinderella just KNEW he would.

Now I can go to the fancy dress ball!

Be warned, darling! Your ninja outfit will turn back to rags at midnight!

Soon...

I am here for the fancy dress ball! May I enter?

Of course you may. Your costume is awesome!

And these are my daughters, Your Highness. They are both old enough to be married, I might add.

I just remembered that I, um, have something to do somewhere else.

Where is he going, I wonder?

WAKE UP.

You're useless. Get up and do your housework.

KNOCK KNOCK!

Hello. I am going to every house in search of the girl who owns this sword.

And so the prince asked the sisters to try it out.

And Ninja-rella protected the prince happily ever after.

The End!

# ALL ABOUT THE ORIGINAL TALE!

The story of Cinderella
has been around for ages.
The first popular version of
the tale was *Cenerentola* by
Giambattista Basile, published in 1634.
This Italian tale tells the story of a widowed
prince who has a daughter called Zezolla (Cinderella) who
convinces her father to marry her nanny. After the wedding, the
nanny moves in with all six of her own daughters. The stepsisters
treat Zezolla like their own personal slave, making the girl
miserable.

While travelling, Zezolla's father meets a magical fairy who gives
presents to him for Zezolla. He gives her a golden spade and bucket,
a silk napkin, and a small tree. Zezolla plants the tree and cares for it.
One day, a magical fairy emerges from its branches. To thank Zezolla
for taking care of her home, the fairy dresses Zezolla in beautiful
clothes and slippers so she can attend the king's royal ball.

At the ball, the king falls in love with Zezolla at first sight, but she
runs away before the king can find out who she is. Eventually, the
king's servant discovers one of Zezolla's slippers that she left behind.
So the king invites all of the ladies in the land to try on the special
shoe. When Zezolla draws near, the shoe jumps from the king's hand
onto her foot. They marry and live happily ever after.

Charles Perrault's version of the tale, *Cendrillon*, was written in 1697.
It includes the following additions: a magical fairy godmother, a
pumpkin-turned-carriage, and special slippers made of glass instead
of fabric!

It's likely that Perrault's additions to
the tale made it more popular.
Now, most adaptations use
his version of the tale,
including this one.

# A **FAR OUT** GUIDE TO NINJA-RELLA'S TALE TWISTS!

Instead of wanting to marry the prince, Ninja-rella wants to be his bodyguard.

The fairy godmother of old is replaced by a fairy godninja, of course.

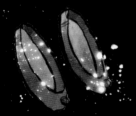  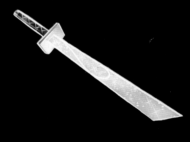

Instead of glass slippers, Ninja-rella gets a special glass katana sword!

And instead of a beautiful gown, Ninja-rella is given an amazing ninja outfit!

**1**

Describe Ninja-rella's appearance in this panel on page 7. How does she feel? How can you tell? If you need help, compare this panel to the final panel on page 6.

**2**

Why are lines extending outwards from the fairy godninja? Why do you think the creators did this? Explain your answer.

**3**

In your own words, describe the path that Ninja-rella travels in this panel.

**4**

How can the prince tell that Ninja-rella's stepsisters aren't the glass sword's owners? Explain your answer.

**5**

The panels on this page are diagonal, or angled to the side. Why did the artist choose to draw the panels like this? How does it make you feel when you read it?

# AUTHOR

**Joey Comeau** is a writer! He lives in Toronto, Canada which is where he wrote the all-ages space-adventure comic *Bravest Warriors*. He also wrote a young adult zombie novel that is pretty spooky.

# ILLUSTRATOR

**Omar Lozano** lives in Monterrey, Mexico. He has always been crazy about illustration and is constantly on the lookout for awesome things to draw. In his free time, he watches lots of films, reads fantasy and sci-fi books, and draws! Omar has worked for Marvel, DC, IDW, Capstone, and several other publishing companies.

# GLOSSARY

**ball** large and extravagant formal party. Some balls, such as fancy dress balls, require all guests to dress as someone else or wear masks.

**bodyguard** person whose job it is to protect someone who is important, such as a queen or a prince

**chess** strategic game played by two people, each with sixteen pieces, on a chessboard. The object of the game is to capture the other player's king.

**godmother** woman who serves as a guardian for a child

**mere** nothing more than what is stated

**ninja** practitioner of the Japanese martial art called ninjutsu. These warriors train to be stealthy and strike quickly

**ruined** destroyed, decayed or spoiled

**stepmother** woman whom your father marries after his marriage to or relationship with your mother has ended. In fairy tales, stepmothers are often unfairly represented as evil and untrustworthy.

**stepsister** daughter of your stepmother or stepfather

**useless** not useful at all, or of no worth or value

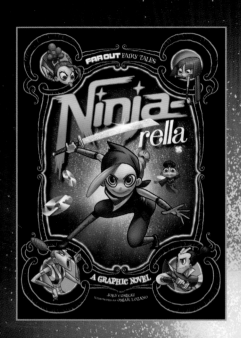
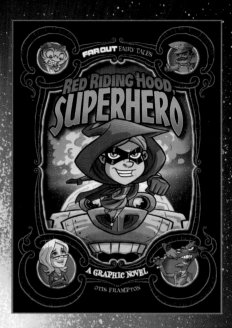
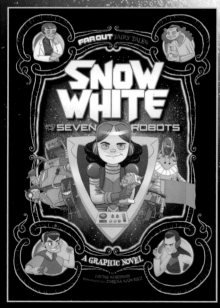
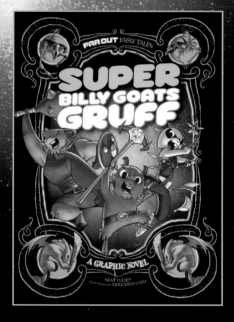